What People Are Saying About *Jackass Letters*

"Jorgensen is the master of yanking corporate American's chain."

-Joel Postman, author of *SocialCorp*-

"In a time when we need real heroes more than ever, Christopher L. Jorgensen arrives to save us all. And I don't care if he masturbates in his kitchen or not—this is not a time to be picky."

-Dave Hill, author of *Tasteful Nudes*-

"In these uncertain times, we need writers like Christopher L. Jorgensen, who aren't afraid to poke the seemingly un-pokeable with an endless arsenal of originality and wit, and discover humanity in the unlikeliest of places."

-Christian Dumais, author of *Smashed: The Life and Tweets of Drunk Hulk*-

"Like the letters your crazy great uncle would write, except twice as coherent, three times as funny, and for the most part legal. The greatest use of the US Postal Service since the SASE!"

-Conor Lastowka, author of *[Citation Needed]*-

Jackass
Letters

Archive Volume 1

Christopher L. Jorgensen

ISBN: 978-0-9978256-6-4
Run Amok Books, 2017

Photo/Illustration Credits

Hoté typing illustration by Anthony Imperioli of Middle Kid
Hoté the Donkey puppet by Mighty Puppets. Photo by Andrea Melendez
Author photo by Aaron Stone Fearless Photography

Contents

FOREWORD

Dear Gentle Reader,

All you need to know about these letters is I wrote them, and I sent them. I put a stamp on stupidity and made the US postal service an unwitting accomplice to idiocy. And I got replies. That's it. I channeled my inner idiot and put his ideas on paper. It's a pretty simple formula, and one anyone can duplicate. Go ahead, I won't mind. In fact, if your letter is good enough I might even let you guest post on *jackassletters.com*. I don't pretend to be original in the idea, or even the execution. Others have done this before me. The hoax letter is a time honored genre, and if you like what I am doing, I encourage you to check out Lazlo Toth and Henry Root. They're better than me. Everyone else is a hack.

Why did I start this project? I like mail. In fact, if you want, you can send a letter to:

Christopher L. Jorgensen
P.O. Box 546
Ames, IA 50010

And I will get it. I can't guarantee I will reply (I try to). So send me a letter, a present, a postcard, or large fat stacks of cash stolen from your mother's purse. Keep your lizards to yourself though. Please.

If you like, skip the rest of this foreword. Like an explanation often ruins a joke, reading anything further runs the risk of taking the fun out of these letters. Don't feel bad. You won't hurt my feelings if you don't read more. You've already paid for the book. I have your money. But for all you fun-haters out there, I thought I would muse a bit on what goes into writing *jackassletters.com*, and why I agreed to allow this book, *Jackass Letters: Archive Volume 1*, to come into being.

You hold in your hands a series of letters I wrote, starting in 2008, along with the replies where possible. These letters are duplicated exactly as they were sent, so writing to tell me about a typo is a waste of time. Those typos were in there and I own them! I thought of changing names to protect the innocent, but my lawyer, Marc J. Randazza, tells me I don't have to, and honestly, who among us is truly innocent? You might not believe some of these letters, or believe I was taken seriously, and that's your right. I won't try to convince you the Earth is round either. For technical reasons we decided to not reproduce scans of the replies in this book, but they are available on the website (assuming the letter is still posted).

So why a book? Writing these sorts of letters amused me, and I want to share them. That's the entirety of my motivation. Originally, I was writing them for myself; an audience of one. But this was singing in the shower. At some point, I decided I needed to share my gift with the world, and others seemed to enjoy them as well, so I created *jackassletters.com*. For nearly a decade this website has served me (and hopefully my readers) well. But while the Internet is a really big place, I can't reach everyone, and not everyone wants to read these letters online. I find I like having an audience, and I want to make it easier for others to access my material. So if Run Amok wants to turn my letters into a book, I figure who am I to say no? I didn't say no.

People ask me if I am trying to effect change in the world. I am not. People ask if I feel guilty for wasting people's time. Again, no. No one is forcing these companies and individuals to engage me, no one even says they have to read my letters. That they do is great, and I get excited every time I get a reply, but at the end of the day, *Jackass Letters* is little more than an outlet for the stupid things that pass through my head. For the most part, I stand behind anything I wrote, though on some occasions I do regret having sent a letter. Sometimes I am an asshole, and sometimes I put this on paper. About the only other thing anyone ever wants to know is whether these letters are supposed to be funny. I don't know. I like humor, so I tried to be funny at least sometimes, but that wasn't always the goal. I'm told they are "friggin' hilarious," but I won't be upset if you don't agree with my lawyer. You can decide for yourself.

Sincerely,

Christopher L. Jorgensen

p.s. When you run a hoax letter site like mine, sometimes people feel compelled to pull my leg. They want to trick the trickster, to prank the prankster. I once even got an offer to be on a reality TV show (yeah, right!). So even after the contract was signed with

Run Amok, I had doubts. The fact that you are holding this book in your hands means this wasn't all some elaborate joke. I think.

*Editor's Note: Most of the Jackass Letters chosen for this volume have responses, which appear alongside them. However, some do not have responses. Those letters have been included simply for your reading pleasure. So enjoy!

For my Mom, the first person to truly appreciate my sense of humor

JACKASS

LETTERS

Archive Volume 1

Christopher L. Jorgensen
P.O. Box 546
Ames, IA 50010

April 21, 2008

The Flying Burrito
2712 Lincoln Way
Ames, Iowa 50014

Dear Flying Burrito,

You make the best mother-fucking burrito I've
ever had.

Thanks,

Christopher L. Jorgensen

Christopher L. Jorgensen
P.O. Box 546
Ames, IA 50010

May 5, 2008

Charmin
c/o Procter & Gamble
1 Procter & Gamble Plaza
Cincinnati, OH 45202

Dear Charmin,

Now that Mr. Whipple is dead, is it OK to squeeze
the Charmin, or is this behavior we should still
avoid?

Thanks,

Christopher L. Jorgensen

The Procter & Gamble
Distributing LLC
PO Box 559
Cincinnati, OH 45201

Dear Mr. Jorgensen,

Thanks for sharing your interest in Mr. Whipple. Here are some interesting facts:

Dick Wilson did commercials for Charmin for many years as George Whipple. His tag line was . . . "Please don't squeeze the Charmin." He passed away November 19, 2007 at the age of 91. Mr. Wilson made more than 500 commercials as Mr. Whipple. He retired in 1985 but P&G brought him back for an encore commercial in 1999. The single ad showed Wilson "coming out of retirement" against the advice of his golfing and poker buddies for one more chance to sell a new Charmin. Thanks for getting in touch with us.

Sincerely,

Carole

Christopher L. Jorgensen
P.O. Box 546
Ames, IA 50010

September 22, 2010

Gorton's, Inc.
128 Rogers Street
Gloucester, Massachusetts 01930

Dear Gorton's, Inc.,

I just saw one of your commercials on TV touting
your Beer Batter Fillets, and I am left with a
question: What kind of beer? I'm a little torn
between hoping it's a really good beer and
hoping you're not wasting good beer. I mean, if
you wouldn't drink it, why would you cook with
it, right? But if you'd drink it, why wouldn't
you just drink it? This make sense? I'd hate to
think that a bunch of beer that would be better
served drunk is going undrunk! Just as I'd hate
to think you guys would use an inferior beer.
I think this is one of those moral dilemmas I
keep hearing about.

Oh yeah, I was also wondering what kind of fish?

Sincerely,

Christopher L. Jorgensen

4

Trusted Since 1849
Gorton's ®
128 Rogers Street,
Gloucester, MA 01930

Dear Christopher,

Thank you for your interest in Gorton's!

Our Beer Batter Fish Fillets are made with high quality beer, sourced from an American beer company. Unfortunately, we are not able to provide detail about the supplier as this information is proprietary. In regards to your question about the type of fish we use in this product, it is Pollock.

We sincerely apologize for the delay in responding to your inquiry. In appreciation of your loyalty, we would like to send you a few coupons redeemable towards your next Gorton's purchase!

Wishing you calm seas,

Your friends at Gorton's

Christopher L. Jorgensen
P.O. Box 546
Ames, IA 50010

July 14, 2011

DSE Healthcare Solutions
164 Northfield Avenue
Edison, NJ 08837 USA

Dear Anti-Monkey Butt Powder,

I have this Canadian friend named Anthony Imperioli,
and I was thinking of sending him some of your
product. Anthony is nearly legally blind and has
quite the hairy hands (if you know what I mean!).
He's constantly complaining about friction burns and
hand fatigue. I asked at my local pharmacy if there
was anything I could send Anthony to alleviate his
discomfort and the old pharmacist recommended
Anti-Monkey Butt Powder. I'm not completely convinced
my leg isn't being pulled!

I'm not sure if Anthony suffers from monkey butt,
and you have to admit there's no good way for one
man to ask another man if his ass is red! (At least
I've found no way to do so. I am open to suggestions.)
So I'm not sure if Anthony needs your product unless
it also aids in the injuries that come from excessive
masturbation. Unless you tell me differently I am
going to assume the answer is no and Anthony will
have to continue to suffer.

On the bright side Anthony is the only Canadian
I know that doesn't need mittens in the winter!

Sincerely,

Christopher L. Jorgensen

6

Christopher L. Jorgensen
P.O. Box 546
Ames, IA 50010

September 13, 2010

Blank Park Zoo
7401 Southwest 9th Street
Des Moines, IA 50315-6667

Dear Blank Park Zoo,

I heard you had a night where people could come
and drink beer and watch the animals getting it
on. Is this true? What night is this and how much
does it cost?

Also, what kind of beer is there?

Sincerely,

Christopher L. Jorgensen

Christopher L. Jorgensen
P.O. Box 546
Ames, IA 50010

September 26, 2012

Peanut Butter & Co.
P.O. Box 2000
New York, NY 10101

Dear Peanut Butter & Co.,

I love peanut butter! I love my girlfriend! Like
chocolate and peanut butter some things just
plain go well together. That's my girlfriend
and I. The only thing that could make things
better would be more peanut butter. I was wondering if there was an easy way to figure out
how much peanut butter would be required to
cover my girlfriend from head to toe. (I don't
want to have to go out for additional jars once
I start this project.) I was thinking a layer
one inch thick, but have to admit I have no
expertise in this area, so don't know what's
optimal.

Would 5 or 10 jars be enough?

Sincerely,

Christopher L. Jorgensen

ALL NATURAL
Peanut Butter & Co
SINCE 1998

November 8, 2012

Dear Christopher L. Jorgensen,

Your letter has been received and it definitely made us chuckle. While peanut butter is our area of expertise we do not have any past experience estimating what you've inquired about.

Hope these coupons can help with the project if you've yet to undertake it.

Good luck,

Isobel de la Fuente
Customer Service

Christopher L. Jorgensen
P.O. Box 546
Ames, IA 50010

October 28, 2011

Vent Haven Museum
33 West Maple Avenue
Fort Mitchell, KY 41011

Dear Vent Haven Museum,

Happy Halloween!

I have a need for a monkey puppet. Can you help
me out? I want to use it to make commentary on
social media. I was going to call it "The Social
Media Monkey," but I have to admit that's not a
very catchy name. My friend Anthony Imperioli
has a puppet. Her name is Nonna Maria and you
have to admit that gives the puppet a bit more
realism. Maybe you could help me out with naming
my monkey puppet too?

I want a monkey puppet so badly that I can taste
it (and we all know how bad puppets taste!). I
want to dress it up in little outfits and play
with it and maybe chase people around. That
would be fun! I also plan to make videos for
the internet featuring the "The Social Media
Monkey!" These would, of course, be inform-
ational and educational and would make the world
a better place, so if you can help me out you'll
be helping the world!

I anxiously await your reply.

Sincerely,

Christopher L. Jorgensen

VENT HAVEN MUSEUM INC.
33 West Maple Ave.
Fort Mitchell, Kentucky 41011

November 12, 2011

Dear Mr. Jorgensen,

Thank you for your letter and interest in ventriloquial puppets. Unfortunately, the museum does not have puppets to sell, so I will not be able to help you out with acquiring a figure. I can suggest, if you are looking for a basic, beginner puppet, you might find one at your local toy store as they usually carry a variety of animal puppets. For a more professional figure you might want to do a Google search of ventriloquist puppets and you will find quite a few companies that sell them.

Good luck searching for your perfect figure! I am sure you will greatly enjoy performing with it and bringing a smile to people's faces.

Sincerely,

Jennifer Dawson, Curator
Vent Haven Museum

Christopher L. Jorgensen
P.O. Box 546
Ames, IA 50010

April 21, 2008

Alpo
c/o Nestle Purina PetCare Company
Customer Services
Checkerboard Square
St. Louis, MO 63164

Dear Alpo,

As you know, with the current state of the
economy and the declining American dollar, many
people on fixed incomes face hard choices about
how best to spend their retirement checks. Sadly,
an increasing number end up eating Alpo, a
product not intended for human consumption. I
would like you to address this issue.

Won't you please do the responsible thing and
come out with "Alpo for Senior Citizens?" With
a properly blended formula it should not be
difficult to achieve a nutritionally balanced
diet for the elderly.

No more would they be forced to eat food meant
for dogs. Instead, with pride, they could buy
an affordable can of food meeting the best needs
of elder care. After all, why should our pets
fare better than our elders?

I hope you will consider this modest proposal.

Thanks,

Christopher L. Jorgensen

Nestlé Purina PetCare
OFFICE OF CONSUMER AFFAIRS
P.O. BOX 1326
WILKES BARRE, PA 18703-9985

May 5, 2008

Dear Mr. Jorgensen,

Thank you for contacting the Nestlé PetCare Company. We always welcome questions and comments from our consumers.

Pet foods contain no ingredients that are harmful to people when ingested, however, we do not recommend people eating pet food. At this time Purina only manufactures foods for cats and dogs, and do not have any future plans to make human foods. However we will be happy to forward your comments to the appropriate departments for review.

Again, thank you for contacting Nestlé PetCare Company. Please contact our Office of Consumer Affairs in the future if we can provide additional assistance.

Sincerely,

Sandy Seigfried
Pet Advisor

Christopher L. Jorgensen
P.O. Box 546
Ames, IA 50010

September 13, 2010

Century Publishing
P.O. Box 11307
Salt Lake City
UT 84147

Dear Century Publishing,

I'm not gay or anything, but sometimes certain
men have some kind of hold over me. I mean hot
is hot if you know what I mean. Like I have this
Canadian friend who's a bit more attractive than
he should be. If Anthony Imperioli wasn't so
far away, and if we both didn't have girl-
friends, I don't know where things would lead!
This thought keeps me up at night!

So I was wondering if you had any tips on nipping
this burgeoning and burdensome desire right in
the bud! Is there a book I should read that will
help keep my on the straight and narrow (I'm
more worried about the straight part).

Sincerely,

Christopher L. Jorgensen

CENTURY PUBLISHING
P.O. Box 11307
Salt Lake City
UT 84147

September 19, 2010

Dear Christopher,

Thanks for writing to us. We've enclosed a brochure about books that may help you. There are also several websites that have good information:

- www.samesexattraction.org general site

- www.exodusinternational.org for Christians

- www.evergreeninternational.org for LDS (Mormon) Christians

- www.couragerc.net for Catholics

- www.jonahweb.org for Jews

Hope these help!

Larry Richman
Century Publishing

Christopher L. Jorgensen
P.O. Box 546
Ames, IA 50010

April 29, 2008

Anheuser-Busch, Inc.
One Busch Place
St. Louis, MO 63118

Dear Budweiser,

I heard that people who work for your company get a free case of Budweiser beer every month. Is this true? Aren't you worried this will somehow promote alcoholism? Drunks don't make the best workers (or so Human Resources keeps telling me)!

Actually, the more I think about this, the cooler this deal sounds. Anyway I can get in on this action? I don't want to work for Anheuser-Busch, Inc., but a free monthly case of Budweiser beer sounds great. You could just send it to the above address.

The way I figure it, this would save me one of my many trips to Casey's.

Thanks,

Christopher L. Jorgensen

p.s. I really like those clydesdales. They're cool!

Anheuser-Busch, Inc.
One of the Anheuser-Busch Companies
One Busch Place
St. Louis, MO 63118

Dear Mr. Jorgensen,

Thank you for taking the time to contact Anheuser Busch. We truly appreciate your interest in our company.

We'd love to be able to assist in your request. However, Anheuser-Busch is an alcohol beverage company, so we do have a certain social responsibility. So that we may assist you, please provide us with your date of birth, in order to ensure that you are above the legal drinking age.

You may reach us at 1-800-DIAL-BUD (800-342-5283) and provide our Customer Information Specialist with the following reference number, [Redacted], for prompt service. We are available 7 days a week, and our hours of operation are:

Monday — Thursday: 8:00am — 8:00pm CST
Friday: 8:00 am — 10:00pm
Saturday: 12:00pm — 10:00pm
Sunday: 12:00 pm — 6:00pm

Again, thank you for writing to Anheuser-Busch, as well as for your understanding in this matter. We hope to hear from you soon!

Sincerely

Kim Burke
Manager
Customer Relationship Group

Christopher L. Jorgensen
P.O. Box 546
Ames, IA 50010

October 4, 2010

Deadwood Chamber of Commerce & Visitor Bureau
767 Main Street
Deadwood, SD 57732

Dear Deadwood,

I fucking loved "Deadwood." The cocksuckers that canceled that show aught to be fucking shot. Goddamn Hoopleheads. This show is the reason I want to visit your cocksucking town. Don't worry, I don't expect it to be like it is on the TV, what with all the whoring and gambling and people using swearwords like "cunt" and "shit." I think swearing for swearing's sake is crass! I hate bastards that do that!

It would disappoint me greatly if I were to visit your town only to discover it bears no resemblance whatsoever to the Deadwood of old. So what can a peckerhead like me expect upon visiting? What is there to do in Deadwood? Should I bring my own guns or are they provided?

Sincerely,

Christopher L. Jorgensen

Deadwood
Black Hills Territory
National Historic Landmark
Gaming • Museums • History • Recreation

Dear Christopher,

Thanks for your letter. We do agree with you that the Hoopleheads who canceled the show don't know what they're doing; but would hope it doesn't come to gun-fire.

We would love to have you visit our town and although we appreciate your enthusiasm, you will not find the Deadwood that was represented in the HBO series. You CAN expect a beautiful town that always has something going on with casinos, restaurants, hotels and views that won't quit.

We recommend you try to come during one of our special event weekends as they are the most fun you'll have anywhere in the Wild West. I've included a special event calendar and a brochure for you to check things out. You can also visit our website for any information you're looking for: www.deadwood.com.

I've also enclosed a little something we think you might enjoy.

Thanks for the correspondence and we hope to see you in Deadwood soon.

Sincerely,

George Milos
Director
Deadwood Chamber & Visitors Bureau
767 Main Street, Deadwood, SD 57732

Christopher L. Jorgensen
P.O. Box 546
Ames, IA 50010

December 8, 2008

Archbishop of Canterbury Dr. Rowan Williams
Lambeth Palace
London
SE1 7JU

Dear Dr. Rowan Williams,

It's totally cool that you write poetry. Not
enough people do that these days. I am sending
you some of mine to look over. I am including
"Man of God," and "Paramour." You probably won't
like them though. Feel free to let me know what
you think. If you do like them you can include
them in your church newsletter!

Would it be possible for me to get an autographed photo? It would be my first autograph
by a published poet. That would be cool of you!

I'm writing because there's a worldwide
recession going on, with cutbacks, layoffs, and
permanent job losses. This got me to wondering
if the Church of England has had to face such
hardships! I hope not, but if so, I had an idea.
You could start outsourcing prayer.

I know this seems ludicrous on the face or it,
but if you think it through I am sure you will
decide the idea has its merits. Many members of
the Church of England are busy people with
little time for things like prayer, and there
are places like India with lots of people that
need employment. I figure a system could be set
up whereby for a small fee Britons could pay

20

one of these needy people to doing the praying on their behalf.

Money would be funneled into impoverished areas of India, Britons would have more time to do good works instead of just praying, and as an added bonus thousands of Indians could be exposed to your ministries!

It seems like a win all around if you ask me.

Sincerely,

Christopher L. Jorgensen

Paramour
by Christopher L. Jorgensen

For him she dressed as a sexy Bo-Peep,
took him to bed, and let him be a bhaaa-ad sheep.
Because of him her bed will always smell of
butter and future lovers will ask,
"You eat a lot of popcorn in here?
Then there's those photos she'll never live down.

She didn't mind being the good witch,
kind of dug Dorothy, even liked playing the bad,
but the flying monkey bit was too far,
and she said "No!" to the munchkins.
Decency demands a line!

She took the ropes, and the candle wax, and
even the whips.
She played the games and bought the outfits
and for him she found a partner when he said
he wanted a threesome.
Unfortunately, it was his best friend Steven.

For him she learned to like pain,
but not as much as he did.
And she never got the whole toe sucking business,
though she kind of found it pleasing and
surprisingly arousing.
For him she bought a dildo (this brought her to four, but
don't tell).

She let him teach her orgasm, something she'd
learned from "Seventeen" (when she was twelve).
She wore the boots and corsets and wondered
if all men were like this.

She hoped so!

Early on, she decided he was the one, decided she'd do anything
for this man.
No other way to explain the whole pony costume.
And she forgave him when he proudly told their
friends,
"I'm back in the saddle again!"

It was love.

Archbishop of Canterbury
Lambeth Palace
London SE1 7JU

27 January 2009

Dear Mr Jorgensen,

I'm very sorry not to have replied sooner to your letter, but it got a bit buried in the Christmas rush, I'm afraid. I just wanted to say thank you for writing to so kindly. Are you still writing poetry? I thought there was a lot of energy in what you wrote, and in the first poem the way in which you use the blood metaphor and the phrase 'I sell my soul to a god that does not exist' are particularly powerful. The second has some very good stuff, but seems to close at some points to the raw data (for example, the use of a person's name in a poem needs careful thought, and I'm not absolutely sure it's justified here), and reads more like work in progress. But I do hope you'll carry on with the creativity.

Outsourcing prayer? Well, in a way we do it all the time simply by the constant exchange of prayer requests across the world (we have a lot that come in here). What I can't quite get my mind around is paying people to pray; I suspect that God might raise an eyebrow...

Photo enclosed; thank you again and best wishes for the New Year.

Yours sincerely

Rowan Williams

Christopher L. Jorgensen
P.O. Box 546
Ames, IA 50010

July 17, 2008

Big Bird
c/o Sesame Workshop
1 Lincoln Plaza
New York, NY 10023

Dear Big Bird,

Can I get an autographed photo?

Also, I was wondering, do you eat meat? Or are
you a vegetarian? What about fish, chicken, or
pork? This is kinda important.

Thanks,

Christopher L. Jorgensen

Sesame Street
A Creation of Sesame Workshop
One Lincoln Plaza
New York, NY 10023

Dear Friend: How nice of you to write to me. I'm always happy to hear from friends like you. I'm going to keep your letter in my nest with all of my special belongings. In return, I'm sending you my autographed picture as a special thank you.

Thanks for writing to me and being my friend. I hope you will continue to watch me and my friends on Sesame Street.

Lots of Love,

Big Bird

Christopher L. Jorgensen
P.O. Box 546
Ames, IA 50010

April 21, 2008

Cialis
c/o Eli Lilly and Company
Lilly Corporate Center, 893 S. Delaware
Indianapolis, IN 46285

Dear Cialis,

I was on your website researching erectile dis-
function and I came across the following:

"As with any ED tablet, in the rare event of priapism
(an erection lasting more than 4 hours), seek
immediate medical help to avoid long-term injury."

You write this like a 4 hour erection is a bad
thing, so I was wondering what is the longest
time I can safely have one? Also, in the event
that I am required to go to the doctor what's
he going to do for me? Can't I just think of
Margaret Thatcher on a cold day?

I only know of one way to reliably get rid of
an erection and that's to have an orgasm, and
frankly I don't think of my doctor in this way.
I think I'd rather just take care of this in
the privacy of my own kitchen, and not a doctor's
office.

Also, I tried to click on the link to get a free
sample, but it's not working, so could you just
send my sample to the above address?

Gratefully,

Christopher L. Jorgensen

Eli Lilly and Company
Lilly Corporate Center, 893 S. Delaware
Indianapolis, Indiana 46285

April 29, 2008

Dear Mr. Jorgensen:

Thank you for your letter regarding Cialis®. If possible, we would like very much to provide information to you. To discuss your inquiry further, you may call 1-800-LillyRx at your convenience or visit www.lilly.com.

The Lilly Answer Center is available to assist you Monday through Friday from 9 am to 5 pm EDT.

Please be advised that the best source of information for any questions or concerns you may have is your own doctor or healthcare professional. He/she is best able to provide information that is targeted toward your clinical circumstances. As each patient's situation is unique, we cannot provide medical guidance, diagnosis, or treatment recommendations.

Sincerely,

The Lilly Answers Center
ELI LILLY AND COMPANY

Christopher L. Jorgensen
P.O. Box 546
Ames, IA 50010

September 10, 2010

Big Ass Fans HQ
2425 Merchant Street
Lexington KY 40511

Dear Big Ass Fans,

Recently I was in the IKEA store in Minneapolis,
MN, and I looked up and saw a big ass fan that
said "Big Ass Fan" right on it, and I thought,
"Yep, that's a big ass fan alright." This got
me to wondering, what the biggest Big Ass Fan you
make?

Can you send me some information on this? It's
for my idea.

Sincerely,

Christopher L. Jorgensen

p.s. any way I could get one of those foam jack-
asses you have on your site?

BIG ASS FANS®
2425 Merchant Street,
Lexington, KY 40511

Dear Future Fan-atics,

As we continue to grow and (r)evolve, we wanted to take this opportunity to share our complete family of cutting-edge fans. For commercial-specific applications we now offer the Element® and Isis™ fans, while our industrial-grade fans have grown to include Powerfoil ® X™, Pivot™ and Airgo™ — all engineered and manu-factured with our superior commitment to quality. The enclosed brochure gives you a quick glimpse of our energy-saving and comfort-producing line-up, but for more in-depth information, please visit www.bigassfans.com or call us at 877-BIG FANS. We look forward to talking with you soon.

Sincerely,

Your Friends at Big Ass Fans

Christopher L. Jorgensen
P.O. Box 546
Ames, IA 50010

April 22, 2008

Des Moines Art Center
4700 Grand Ave.
Des Moines, IA 50312-2099

Dear Des Moines Art Center,

A while back I went to your Art Center to see
"Habitat Group for a Shooting Gallery" by Joseph
Cornell, but was told it was "on loan." This
seems like a great program to me. I didn't realize you did this.

I am a huge Francis Bacon fan and would like to
borrow, "Study After Velasquez's Portrait of Pope
Innocent X." I have a place above my bed picked
out for it, though admittedly this might upset
the girlfriend. She would rather we get "Automat"
by Edward Hopper. I told her I would ask.

How many can I borrow at a time? If it's only
one I guess we'll take the Hopper (have to keep
the girlfriend happy!). But in this case, any chance
I could buy the Bacon?

If you deliver, just send them to the above
address, or contact me with a good time for us
to pick them up.

Thanks,

Christopher L. Jorgensen

Des Moines Art Center
Edmundson Art Foundation, Inc.
4700 Grand Avenue
Des Moines, Iowa 50312-2099

April 23, 2008

Dear Mr. Jorgensen:

Thank you for your inquiry into the loan of the Des Moines Art Center's work by Joseph Cornell entitled Habitat Group for a Shooting Gallery. I regret that the artwork was out on loan when you visited the museum.

When you visited, Habitat Group for a Shooting Gallery was at the Smithsonian American Art Museum in Washington, D.C. in a major retrospective exhibition of the artist's work where is was seen by thousands of visitors. It is common practice for art museums to lend their works of art to other museums for exhibition projects. This is how the museum field adds to the scholarship of works of art and adds to the cultural record in general. For example, our painting Automat is currently at the Art Institute of Chicago in a major Hopper exhibition, after the exhibition's stop at the Museum of Fine Arts, Boston. Our Francis Bacon painting will soon travel to the Prado Museum in Madrid, The Tate Modern in London, and finally the Metropolitan Museum of Art in New York before it returns to us. Likewise, the Art Center will be borrowing 75 works of art from major museums across the country for an exhibition entitled After Many Springs opening here January 2009.

I hope this give you a better understanding of why this work was not on view during your visit to the Art Center. Please come again.

Best regards,

Jeff Fleming
Director

Christopher L. Jorgensen
P.O. Box 546
Ames, IA 50010

December 17, 2009

Federal Communications Commission
Consumer & Governmental Affairs Bureau
Consumer Inquiries & Complaints Division
445 12th Street, SW
Washington, DC 2054

Re: Support of the American Broadcasting Company
for its American Music Awards broadcast of Adam
Lambert's performance

Dear FCC,

I am writing in support of Adam Lambert's
performance at the American Music Awards and I
applaud ABC for the bravery of the broadcast.
I know some woman named "Anita L. Staver" has
written in with the opposite viewpoint. She's
just a plain wrong thinking individual!

She states:

The Lambert performance featured, among other
things, simulated oral sex, suggestive crotch
grabbing, simulated digital penetration, sado-
masochistic conduct, and homosexual open-mouth
kissing.

Now, at face value I agree with her. As a hetero-
sexual male this is nothing I want to see on my
TV (which I why I am grateful my TV has more
channels than Mrs. Staver's), but I am a fair
minded individual, and must admit some fondness
for girl on girl action.

So while I do not get the appeal of watching Lambert nosh on a dude, I'd totally be there if it was a couple lesbians. Like I said, I am a fair minded man, so seems to me, if it's acceptable for two women to get it on, as much as I may personally find it objectionable, I must also accept two men getting it on.

People have options. There was an easy solution to this situation available to Mrs. Staver. She could have changed the channel, but instead she chose to write your fine organization to complain and ask for fines. Mrs. Staver seems like a sexually repressed and frustrated woman, and I am sorry she was forced to watch Lambert's performance, but the fact that she is seeking to redefine what is acceptable on TV is disconcerting to me. I do not want people like her making decisions about what I am allowed to see. Please do not give this women this power or she interfere with my God given right to watch lesbians making out.

This letter is an adaptation of FCC Form 27b/6.

Sincerely,

Christopher L. Jorgensen

Christopher L. Jorgensen
P.O. Box 546
Ames, IA 50010

July 20, 2011

Bon Ami Company
1025 W. 8th Street
Kansas City, MO 64101-1200

Dear Bon Ami,

I'm a lot like Gomez Addams. Dashingly handsome,
stylish, clever and witty, decent with a rapier,
and possessing a profound weakness for French.
In fact the other day my girlfriend was cleaning
the kitchen, being all domestic in her apron
and scrubbing the coffee-stained sink (I've
since been admonished to pour coffee directly
into the drain). I asked what she was doing and
she said something like "bon ami," so after I
was done showering her with kisses, and I recov-
ered my senses, I went to the internet to find
out what "bon ami" meant. I think you can understand I was bit disappointed to find out it just
means "good friend." Oh well.

The girlfriend loves your scouring powered.
(Apparently not enough to allow me to continue
pouring coffee in the sink.) Maybe some day I'll
buy an apron and give it a go!

Sincerely,

Christopher L. Jorgensen

BON AMI COMPANY
1025 West 8th Street
Kansas City, MO 64101-1200

August 2, 2011

Dear Mr. Jorgensen:

Thank you for your complimentary email regarding your experience with our Bon Ami Powder Cleanser. It's always a pleasure to read favorable correspondence from one of our customers. We are proud of the high quality of our products and we appreciate you taking the time to provide us with some feedback.

As a thank you for your continued support and loyalty to our products, several money saving offers for your next in store purchases are enclosed. In appreciation of your amusing letter, I also enclosed a Bon Ami baby chick. Perhaps a snuggly trinket you may give to your lady friend?

Again, thank you for taking the time to write us. For over 120 years, Faultless Starch/Bon Ami Company has guaranteed complete customer satisfaction with all of our products. Should you have any other questions or suggestions, please feel free to contact us again.

Sincerely,

Renee
Consumer Specialist

Christopher L. Jorgensen
P.O. Box 546
Ames, IA 50010

December 10, 2010

Exotic Feline Rescue Center
2221 E. Ashboro Road
Center Point, IN 47840

Dear Exotic Feline Rescue Center,

Merry Christmas!Every year around this time my
thoughts turn to Christmas, which then makes me
think of Jesus, which makes me think of Christians, which makes me think of lions, and then I
smile.

I looked at your gift store online and didn't see
what I wanted, but I decided to send you $20 anyway.
What would make my day is a lucky lion's tooth (or
bobcat or leopard or cougar, pretty much anything
except an ocelot's, since who'd want one of those?).
I'm not suggesting someone go pull a lion's tooth
just to send me one, but I figure these cats probably
lose teeth all the time! But maybe they don't. Maybe
they have better dental plans than your typical
American, in which case, I guess you don't have to
send me anything.

Since you made me smile I am sending along $20
(it's the same as in town!). Keep up the good work.

Sincerely,

Christopher L. Jorgensen

p.s. if a tooth is out of the question I'd take
a claw if one of the lions is done with his.

Exotic Feline Rescue Center
2221 East Ashboro Road
Center Point, IN 47840

TAX RECEIPT

Thank you for your recent gift to the Exotic Feline Rescue Center. We value your continued support and all the many wonderful things it makes possible. As we continually strive toward providing the best possible care and environment for all our exotic big cats, it is through gifts such as yours that we are able to thrive as an organization dedicated to the rescue and care of these magnificent animals. We thank you again and look forward to your continued support.

Joe Taft
Founder/Director

2010 TAX RECEIPT

Name: C. Jorgensen
Address: PO Box 546
Ames, IA 50010
Date Gift Received: 12/2010
Gift Amount: $20.00

Christopher L. Jorgensen
P.O. Box 546
Ames, IA 50010

July 6, 2011

Blairex Laboratories, Inc.
1600 Brian Drive P.O. Box 2127
Columbus, IN 47202-2127

Dear Boudreaux's Butt Paste,

I have this Canadian friend named Anthony
Imperioli who acts all butt hurt all the time.
He's a sensitive guy and the slightest thing sets
him off. There's nothing worse than when a Canadian
Italian man turns on the waterworks! Anyway, I was
thinking of sending him a tub of your butt
paste, but I am afraid it will get confiscated
by overzealous border agents determined to keep
Canada safe from wayward butt paste.

Mind you, I don't know if he has an actual need
for the stuff (it wouldn't surprise me if their
socialized medicine gives out free butt paste),
but I was thinking sending him some butt paste
would make the perfect point and maybe get him
to man up a bit (the man shaves his chest for
jimminy's sake!). I'm guessing it'll backfire
and he'll end up crying about getting a tub of
butt paste. (I plan to still do it though).

I'd like to send him the biggest tub you have. What
size would this be? I'm thinking anything over a 5
gallon bucket would be cost prohibitive to mail, but
I might still consider it if you have larger.

Sincerely,

Christopher L. Jorgensen

The largest Butt Paste size is a 16oz plastic tub.
Thank you

Christopher L. Jorgensen
P.O. Box 546
Ames, IA 50010

January 24, 2013

50 State Security Service, Inc
915 NE 125th Street, Ste.
106 North Miami, FL 33161

Dear 50 State Security,

I would like a job application. I believe I am
probably qualified for the job, and I am tired
of Iowa winters! Please send to the above address.

Most days I am quite content with my lot in
life. I've most of Maslow's hierarchy of needs
met (though I am still working on that whole
"respect of others" thing). I am only a few
steps from becoming self-actualized. In short,
I do suffer from a defect in morality. It's not
that I am a bad person, I just tend to want to
do bad things to bad people. In my mind this
puts me on the side of the righteous! I am sort
of like Saint Augustine, "Da mihi castitatem et
continentiam, sed noli modo!" To this end I've
always wanted to be a cop. I tried, but apparently I am too smart to be police. I scored too
high on the IQ exam and was told I would be
bored with the job. Personally, I think they
underestimated my ability to amuse myself!

While security is my second choice I still feel
I would be good at it. Sure, I won't be a
homicide detective or anything, but I can stop
spending weekends as a costumed vigilante, and
instead become a professional security officer
(with a real paycheck!). I can't wait to start

keeping the unruly citizens of Florida in line!
My references are available upon request.

I only have two questions: Do you offer relocation
assistance? What kind of gun will be provided?

Sincerely,

Christopher L. Jorgensen

Christopher L. Jorgensen
P.O. Box 546
Ames, IA 50010

December 7, 200

Santa Claus
1 Santa Claus Lane
North Pole, AK 99705

Dear Santa,

My dad says I can only write if I "make it very clear" I am "an over privileged person who is too old to be writing Santa." He's afraid someone will send a toy that could go to some deserving kid, and he's right. I haven't been very good this year, so anything sent to me will just be donated. So why am I writing? Well, I have a question.

What does Santa call the "elves?" "Santa's Little Helpers" doesn't sound very nice and everyone knows there are no such thing as elves (or fairies either, even tooth ones). Calling an elf small or little seems like bullying to me and I know that bullying is bad, so what does Santa call them? Some of my friends want to know really really bad, so I said I would ask.

What does Santa call the elves?

Thanks,

Christopher L. Jorgensen

p.s. I turn ██ in August! Dad says I can't tell!

Santa's Mail Bag
1 Santa Claus Lane
North Pole, Alaska 99705

Dear C. Jorgenson

Merry Christmas

From Santa,

You have been so good this year that I am writing this letter especially for you.

I just finished making the last toys for the year. Now the elves will put all those toys in my sleigh. It's a big, big job and the elves work very hard. I'm sure you work very hard too.

I'll be checking my list again, I always check it twice, to see who has been naughty or nice. You are on the good list and Santa hopes you will continue to be good all the time.

Some of the younger elves are learning how to take care of the reindeer. They can't do it by themselves yet, but they are learning. They are good helpers, just like you.

Santa wishes you a very Merry Christmas.

Elf Ricky

Christopher L. Jorgensen
P.O. Box 546
Ames, IA 50010

January 31, 2012

Campbell Soup Company
1 Campbell Place
Camden, NJ 08103

Dear Campbell's Soup,

I think you should come out with duck soup. Duck
is probably my favorite bird to eat (I've never
had egret though). Duck & Dumplings, Duck & Noo-
dles, Duck Vegetable. I'm salivating just thinking about it (it'll make sealing this letter
that much easier!)!

A friend of mine told me you sell watercress
and duck gizzard soup in China, but I'm not sure
I believe him. The duck gizzard isn't exactly
something I'd be excited about eating. I'm also
not going to go all the way to China to get a
can of soup, so please come out with duck soup
in America, but make sure it's the tasty parts!

I want me some duck! M'm! M'm! Good!

Sincerely,

Christopher L. Jorgensen

Campbell's ®
Consumer Response Center
One Campbell Place
Camden, NJ 08103-1701

February 9, 2012

Dear Mr Jorgensen:

We have forwarded your comments to the appropriate department. We appreciate feedback like yours because it helps us become aware of consumer preferences and concerns.

At Campbell, our number one priority is to delight our consumers. We realize that it is consumers like you who have helped build our businesses and we sincerely appreciate your loyalty.

As a small token of our thanks, I've enclosed a coupon. Please use it to enjoy your favorite product from the Campbell family of brands including V8, Prego, Pace, and Pepperidge Farm.

Sincerely,

Dreena Toporcer
Consumer Services Representative

Christopher L. Jorgensen
P.O. Box 546
Ames, IA 50010

October 14, 2009

Matt Nadeau
Rock Art Brewery LLC
254 Wilkins St.
Morrisville,VT 05661

Dear Matt Nadeau,

Monster Energy Drink sucks balls! I just thought
I'd get that out there.

First, find $5 enclosed to help out. You can throw
it into your legal defense fund, your Matt Nadeau
beer drinking fund, or buy your wife something
special (I don't care). I just hope it helps.

Second, you know that song "99 Bottles of Beer
on the Wall?" Well, how do you think they got
them up there? I mean, what's the best way to
affix a beer to a wall? This one has vexed me
for a long time, so I figured since I was writing
you anyway, I'd go ahead and ask an expert. On
a related note, how many of my friends do I have
to invite over to responsibly "take them down
and pass them around?" I was thinking three, but
can tell Marty to stay home if this is too many.
What do you think?

Third, if you ever feel like making a "Christopher
L. Jorgensen" beer, don't worry, I won't sue you!

Sincerely,

Christopher L.
Jorgensen

p.s. I went to high school with a Holly Nadeau.
Do you know what she's been up to?

enc. $5

Hi Christopher,

Happy Holidays
From Your Friends at
Rock Art Brewery

Matt, Rich, Renee,
ZF, Jessyca, Andrea

p.s. We don't know a Holly Nadeau

Christopher L. Jorgensen
P.O. Box 546
Ames, IA 50010

July 29, 2011

French Meadow Bakery
1000 Apollo Road
Eagan, MN 55121

Dear French Meadow Bakery,

There's a good chance my girlfriend just ate one of your
cakes that was four months old. After she'd been gnawing
on this thing for days we looked on the bottom of the
box and there is a sticker that says 0316. Does that
stand for March 16? As you can see from the date of this
letter it is July 28, 2011. Four months seems like a
long time for a cake to be good. Heck, since there's no
year this cake could be 16 months old or older! There's
also a chance that that sticker means nothing, that it's
just put on the box to confuse people like me.

So we went on your website to get clarification. We
wanted to see if there was information about how long
your cakes are edible, or what that sticker means, but
we don't even see cakes listed at all! (Though there
is a tasty picture of one.) We put in our zip code and
it said you don't sell them anywhere near us, so have
you discontinued this product?

You might want to let the Hy-Vee in Ames, IA know they are
selling four month old cakes if this ends up being the case,
and I'll let you know if my girlfriend ends up getting sick.

Sincerely,

Christopher L. Jorgensen

48

French Meadow Bakery
1000 Apollo Road
Eagan, MN 55121

Hello Christopher,

Thank you for contacting French Meadow Bakery. It sounds like the cake was old. Was it frozen when you purchased it?

The cake was made on November 12, 2010 but has a 9 month frozen shelf life. Please feel free to call us with any questions (651-286-7891) & try another product on us.

In Health,
Emily

Christopher L. Jorgensen
P.O. Box 546
Ames, IA 50010

February 11, 2011

Georgia-Pacific Consumer Products
133 Peachtree St., N.E.
Atlanta, GA 30303

Dear Georgia-Pacific,

The other day I was getting out a fresh roll of
toilet paper and I noticed on the side of the
box it says, "Now EPA Complaint." I'm a huge
fan of buying bulk (mostly because I am cheap!),
but I'm a bit concerned. If this said "EPA
Compliant" I wouldn't be worried, but the addi-
tion of that "Now" makes it seem as though pre-
viously my bathroom tissue was not compliant
with the Environmental Protection Agency. What
was wrong with it before?

Obviously my primary concern is where I've been
putting this product. Wiping various areas with
tissue that is environmentally unfriendly is
troublesome at best. I only want the highest quality anywhere near there! Part of me wants to say
that the EPA should have nothing to do with what
I choose to use to wipe with, but another part of
me thinks we need an agency to govern just such
a thing!

Well, congratulations on your recent EPA compli-
ance. I still want to know what was wrong with
your toilet paper before.

Sincerely,

Christopher L. Jorgensen

GP Georgia-Pacific
Georgia-Pacific Consumer Products LP
Consumer Response Department
P.O. Box 105141
Atlanta, GA 30348-5141

March 31, 2011

Dear Mr. Jorgensen:

Thank you for contacting the Georgia-Pacific Consumer Response Center. Georgia-Pacific places tremendous importance on the feedback we receive from our consumers.

We require additional information in order to assist you. Please contact us at 1-800-2TellGP, Monday through Friday, 9am to 5pm est. or respond to this email with the following:

Your Case #743097
Full Name of Product and Size of Package
Proof of Purchase Code (located above and/or below the bar code)
Core Code (letters and numbers printed inside of cardboard roll)
Store in which you purchased the product

We will be happy to take care of this and appreciate you bringing it to our attention.

Sincerely,

Andrea

Christopher L. Jorgensen
P.O. Box 546
Ames, IA 50010

April 12, 2011

Simply Asian Foods, LLC
2342 Stattuck Ave.
PMB #322
Berkeley, CA 94704-4242

Dear Simply Asian Foods,

I find your noodle bowls to be quite tasty and
satisfying. The only complaint I have is the
fork. At first I thought you were including an
authentic Asian fork with the meal (and this is
why it's so small), but then I realized that the
Asians would be eating these bowls with chop-
sticks! The portion size could be a bit bigger
as well, and I like mine a bit more spicy, but
other than these things I love the noodle bowls.

Could you please ship these bowls with a
caucasian sized fork?

Sincerely,

Christopher L. Jorgensen

Simply Asian Foods, LLC
2342 Stattuck Ave.
PMB #322
Berkeley, CA 94704-4242

June 9, 2011

Dear Jorgenson:

Thank you for taking the time to contact us. We welcome the opportunity to address your disappointing experience with our Simply Asia Spicy Mongolian Noodle Soup Bowls. We have forwarded your comments about thr fork to our Marketing Department for review

We apologize for any inconvenience that you may have experienced. Please accept the enclosed with our compliments. If we can be of further assistance, please call us at 1-800-967-8424, Monday through Friday, 9:30AM to 9PM, and weekends 11AM to 7PM Eastern Time. We hope to have the continued pleasure of serving you.

Best Regards,

Mary Lepley
Consumer Affairs Specialist

Christopher L. Jorgensen
P.O. Box 546
Ames, IA 50010

August 15, 2011

Cockapoo Club of America
PO Box 2
Christmas Valley, Oregon 97641

Dear Cockapoo Club of America,

My friend Anthony Imperioli wants both a cocker
spaniel and a poodle. Unfortunately he can't
have both with his prior track record of not
being able to care for more than one pet at a
time (don't even ask about the miniature don-
keys!), so I suggested he get a cockapoo! At
first he wouldn't believe there was any such
thing, but when I showed him pictures he
instantly fell in love! Thing is, he really
prefers the cocker spaniel to the poodle, so
was wondering if some cockatoos come with more
cock and less poo. I figured you'd be the best
people to answer this question.

Please let me know at your earliest convenience.

Sincerely,

Christopher L. Jorgensen

Cockapoo Club of America, Inc.
P. O. Box 2, Christmas Valley, Oregon 97641
August 22, 2011

Dear Christopher,

Yes some cockapoo's can have more the Cocker spaniel appearance.
Most generally you will see the cocker appearance in a second
generation. Once in a while in a first or third. But Yes there is defiantly
a difference. Some can have the Cocker appearance, the poodle
appearance and then the preferred look the Benji Look.

I have a black second generation male that was one year in May that
has more the cocker appearance. I have him on special for $250.00
+ shipping. He is already neutered and current on all his shots.

Hope this helps
All my best

Debbie Cowdrey
President, Cockapoo Club of America

Christopher L. Jorgensen
P.O. Box 546
Ames, IA 50010

October 13, 2009

Marc J. Randazza, PA
P.O. Box 5516
Gloucester, Massachusetts 01930

Dear Marc J. Randazza,

I loved how you took Glenn Beck to task and exposed
him for the idiot he is. This was sheer brilliance!
You, sir, are now my idol. This is a great and
terrible thing, so I thought I'd write and let you
know your responsibilities.

1. You must keep on being awesome. Failure to do
so will will only result in disappointment in my
life and frankly I've had enough of this.
2. You must send me an autographed photo for my
shrine. I know this must be a common request for
most lawyers, what with their adoring legions
of fans and all, but for you it is a requirement.
You can send the photo to the above address.
3. There really isn't a third thing, but two
things makes a pretty short and lame list. Be
awesome and the photo does pretty much covers it!

If you do this, I will light a candle in your honor
whenever I am in a church that allows this (for at
least the next year or until I find a new idol or you
quit being awesome, whatever comes first). Also, I'll
let you defend me against Glenn Beck when he sues me!

Sincerely,

Christopher L. Jorgensen

p.s. I don't really have anything more to say, but I
like post scripts.

56

Marc J. Randazza, PA
P. O. Box 5516
Gloucester, Massachusetts 01930

October 21, 2009

Dear Christopher L. Jorgensen,

Thank you for recognizing my awesomeness. I am pleased to accept your request to serve as your idol. I will continue to be awesome to my best of ability, as I would not wish to disappoint you. Your letter states that you have had enough disappointment, and as your idol I would like to use my awesomeness to push your life in another direction. From now on, you shall have nothing but awesomeness in your life if I have anything to say about it.

I would like to request that you not light candles in my honor, at least not in any churches. I am an atheist, and I think that churches are definitely not awesome. If you light a candle in one (in my honor), and then it falls over and burns the church down, people might think that I put you up to it. So lets be careful with fire, young Christopher!

You strike me as a very special boy and a key member of the Randazza Society. I wish I could come visit in Iowa and assist you with your work.

Finally, I would not worry about Glenn Beck suing you. He is an asshat, and by the time you get this letter, he will probably have already self-destructed like Morton Downey Junior. Do you remember him? Don't worry. Nobody else does either.

Your friend,

Attorney Marc J. Randazza
Dictated, but not read.

p.s. There isn't really a "Randazza Society," but it sounds like a good idea to start one. You are its number one and founding member.

Christopher L. Jorgensen
P.O. Box 546
Ames, IA 50010

July 27, 2013

Chipotle Mexican Grill, Inc.
1401 Wynkoop St., Ste. 500
Denver, CO 80202

Dear Chipotle Mexican Grill,

I've never eaten in one of your stores, but then I've never really had a reason to until recently! Yesterday I heard tell of a thing called a "quesarito" and this gave me pause. It was describes as a quesadilla wrapped around a burrito. Two layers of tortillas with cheese between them surrounding the contents of a burrito! It would take unicorn meat to make this thing sound any more perfect. (I am salivating as I write this!)

I am normally quite a skeptic. I don't believe anything I can't verify on the internet, and surprisingly, the internet says this is true! (I haven't checked snopes yet though.) So I feel a bit silly even asking about the quesarito, but I have to know how one goes about ordering this thing. Is there a secret handshake (and if there is will the employee wash his hands after)? How much can I be expected to pay?

Unfortunately, the internet says there is no such thing as unicorn meat, so I suppose I will get chicken, but with enough cheese I think I can get by! Just let me know how to go about ordering this bad boy!

Sincerely,

Christopher L. Jorgensen

CHIPOTLE MEXICAN GRILL, INC.
1401 WYNKOOP STREET, SUITE 500
DENVER, CO 80202

April 7, 2013

Dear Christopher,

Thanks for writing in. My name is Nathan and I work with our Customer Service team in the corporate office. I can say that here at Chipotle we strictly prohibit the killing and/or use of Unicorn meat in any of our food. With this being said, the Quesoritto is a real thing that has caught a fire as of recently. Though you may not find it on our menu, you may order by first singing the Quesoritto song, followed by the Quesoritto dance. Or, you can always just ask for it and our team members should know how to make it. If they are confused, walk them through it and I promise they will help you get that magical burrito just as you want it. Depending on how you order it, the charge my vary. if you use only a single tortilla (i.e. cheese melted on the inside of your burrito) the charge is the same as a burrito. If you choose to use two tortillas, expect to pay for both the quesadilla and the burrito.

Best of luck on your quest for the Quesoritto. We wish you all the best in your wonderful journey.

Sincerely,

Nathan
Customer Service
Chipotle Mexican Grill

P.S. Please don't eat Unicorn meat. That's not cool.

Christopher L. Jorgensen
P.O. Box 546
Ames, IA 50010

October 25, 2010

Car Talk Plaza
Box 3500 Harvard Square
Cambridge, MA 02238

Dear Car Talk Guys,

First off, can I get an autographed photo of one
or both of you?

I also have a few questions, and you're my last
best hope. I already asked the Ringling Brothers,
but I guess those guys are too busy, so I thought
I'd ask you instead, since I know you'll have
the time!

I am interested in becoming a clown. Even my
best friends consider me to be a jackass, I
don't mind makeup that much, and I do like some
kids, so I think it might be a good fit.

My girlfriend insists some men compensate for
a lack of equipment (if you know what I mean)
by driving large cars like a Ford Mustang or a
GM Hummer. I tried to reassure her this is why I
drive a 2000 Dodge Neon, but this just scared her.

Anyway, this leaves me with three questions: 1,
how many clowns can fit in a 2000 Dodge Neon?
2, what is the average size of a clown's unit?
3, Do I have to send you any kind of picture to
prove I can fit in a clown car?

I am just wondering if I should reconsider my
career choices.

Sincerely,

Christopher L. Jorgensen

p.s. If you're interested I can send along a
picture of my "resume" (if you know what I mean).

Christopher L. Jorgensen
P.O. Box 546
Ames, IA 50010

July 20, 2011

Blair Lazar
PO Box 363
Highlands, NJ 07732

Dear Blair's Death Rain,

Holy shit man! My mouth is on fire. I was only
able to make it through one ounce of a two ounce
bag of your Habanero Kettle Cooked Potato Chips.
To be fair though I had absolutely nothing to
drink. No water, no milk, no beer, no soda pop!
You should consider saying a two once bag is
two servings. That way I wouldn't have to feel
as bad about letting a bag of potato chips unman
me. I think I could have made a better showing
for myself if I wasn't breathing the Habanero
dust off the chips.

Balls! These things are hot. I love hot stuff
that has flavor. These also have a great flavor.
It's too easy to just make something hot, but
you give these chips fire and taste! I love them.

My girlfriend thinks I have burned off all my
taste buds. I try to tell her I can taste things
she can't. My palate is super sensitive. She
never believes me. I'm going to buy some of your
hot sauces now. I hope they are as flavorful as
your chips!

Sincerely,

Christopher L. Jorgensen

Blair's Deathsauce
Gardner Resources
Highlands
NJ 07732

From the desk of Blair

Hello Christopher,

Great to get a real letter! These days the E-world moves so fast people just hit send!

Feel alive

Your chilipal

Blair

Christopher L. Jorgensen
P.O. Box 546
Ames, IA 50010

September 1, 2011

NASA Headquarters
Suite 5K39
Washington, DC 20546-0001

Dear NASA,

Since you're not going to be launching anymore
shuttles I think you should do something else to
keep people's attention. I propose you shoot
another monkey into space! This would be fun and
can't be that expensive. I bet people would become
avid followers of this space monkey. You could
make a twitter feed for it and a Facebook page
and a YouTube channel and stuff and people could
watch the monkey's every move!

I know I'd pay attention. While this wouldn't be
anything new (we've had monkeys in space before)
it has been long enough since the last monkeyed
flight that this would at least be novel!

If you're not interested in doing this I was
hoping you could send along some suggestions
about how I might try this on my own. I'm pretty
sure I can come up with the monkey if you know where
I can get a rocket I think I'll be set! I'd rather
leave this to the professionals though so please
consider doing this. I think it would be great!

You should name the monkey Yuri.

Sincerely,

Christopher L. Jorgensen

NASA Headquarters
Washington, DC 20546-0001

Dear Mr. Jorgensen:

This is in response to your letter of Sept 1, 2011.

The President's fiscal year 2011 budget request provides for expanding NASA's climate research and aeronautics program which emphasizes the Next Generation Air Transportation System, continuing the strong space science program, enabling transformative technology essential to human exploration, and significant support for commercial spaceflight services to low-Earth orbit.

You may have had the opportunity to hear President Obama on April 15, 2010, during his visit to NASA's Kennedy Space Center. He talked directly to the issues you raise. NASA's Constellation Program is being restructured and the Space Shuttle fleet will be retired. The President believes that the space program needs new direction, and he declared, that by 2025, we will send humans to land on an asteroid. He also stated, "By the mid-2030's, I believe we can send humans to orbit Mars and return them safely to Earth. Landing on Mars will follow, and I expect to be around to see it."

NASA is committed to exploration with both humans and robots. This new direction will change the way NASA does things, but will not change what the Agency does. There is nothing in this new path that precludes NASA from sending humans to the Moon, Mars, or elsewhere. In fact, it provides for the technologies required to do so, and NASA embraces the opportunity to build the infrastructure for a long-term sustainable spacefaring Nation.

Thank you for your interest in NASA.

Sincerely,

Public Communications Program
Public Outreach Division
Office of Communications

Christopher L. Jorgensen
P.O. Box 546
Ames, IA 50010

November 27, 2009

Ferrara Pan Candy Company
7301 W. Harrison Street
Forest Park, IL 60130

Dear Lemonhead,

This should come as no surprise, but I love your candy! In fact, it's my second favorite candy of all time (I have to admit a greater weakness for French Burnt Peanuts), but I have a a couple questions. 1.) Why is "Lemonhead" singular and not plural? After all, there are more than one in a box. Actually, there's usually quite a generous amount. 2.) Why is there "Nutrition Facts" on the side of the box? This seems silly to me since as far as I can tell Lemonhead(s) meet no nutritional needs, and I'm OK with that, since who eats them for their nutritional value? Dumb people. I eat them because they taste yummy!

I have to admit I love smuggling a box of Lemonhead(s) into a movie theater. Do you think this makes me a bad person? Sometimes I feel like I am stealing from the theater, but then who in his right mind would pay movie theater prices for a box of candy? If anyone is stealing it the movie theater? I suppose the type of people that pay these prices are the same people who expect candy to be nutritional. Dumb people. This is why I choose to smuggle them.

Anyway, keep on making a great product!

Sincerely,

Christopher L. Jorgensen

Ferrara Pan Candy Co.
7301 West Harrison Street
Forest Park, Illinois 60130-2083

Christopher L. Jorgensen
PO Box 546
Ames, IA 50010

December 4, 2009

Dear Mr. Jorgensen:

Thank you for your letter. We are always pleased to hear from our customers and know they enjoy eating our candy as much as we enjoy making it. Lemonhead is singular as it refers to the Lemonhead character on the package. As for the nutrition facts, we are required by law to include nutrition information on all products we sell.

We hope that you will continue to purchase our products and find the quality and taste to your satisfaction.

Sincerely,

Salvatore Ferrara II
President/CEO

Christopher L. Jorgensen
P.O. Box 546
Ames, IA 50010

December 9, 2008

Governor Arnold Schwarzenegger
State Capitol Building
Sacramento, CA 95814

Dear Governor Arnold Schwarzenegger,

Could I please get an autographed photo for my
girlfriend? Just make it out to "███████."

Also, I was wondering do you ever say "to crush
your enemies, see them driven before you, and to
hear the lamentation of the women" anymore? I bet
that would drive the Democrats absolutely nuts!

Thanks,

Christopher "It's not a tumor!" Jorgensen

Office of the Governor
Governor Arnold Schwarzenegger
Sacramento, California 95814
February 4, 2009

Dear Mr. Jorgensen,

Thank you for your letter requesting my photo. I always appreciate hearing from my supporters and fans. As Governor, I've been honored by the number of well-wishers who have taken the time to write me.

I have enclosed a photo for your collection, with my compliments. Again, thank you for your correspondence.

Sincerely,

Arnold Schwarzenegger

Christopher L. Jorgensen
P.O. Box 546
Ames, IA 50010

December 1, 2012

Maple Leaf Farms, Inc.
P.O. Box 308
Milford, Indiana 46542-0308

Dear Maple Leaf Farms,

I love duck, but I am not sure I should be allowed near one (alive or dead). When I was in high school I decided to cook one for my prom date. I popped that sucker in the oven for a full hour before we ate it. That duck was pretty bloody and barely warm in places. I'm sure I had the temperature incorrect, but we ate it anyway. I survived. I believe my date did as well, but to this day I am not sure. She may have used me for a one night duck. The next day (and for ever after) she never returned my phone calls. I prefer to think she wasn't some kind of a trollop, but the alternative means I may have unintentional committed manslaughter, since she never came back to class either.

That was over 20 years ago. I've moved on. Hopefully, so have the statues of limitations and her parents! (They had other kids.)

The other night I roasted my second duck, a Maple Leaf Farms duck, one of your ducks, a fine duck (if you ask me), but I may have overcooked it this time! I think I started out with a six pound duck, but after cooking I bet that thing weighed less than your average chicken! Since it's four times as expensive as your average chicken this is not what I wanted.

What did I do wrong? Was three hours too long?

In another 20 years, when I am close to retiring,
I was thinking I would try again. I would like
your advice on duck...and perhaps women.

Sincerely,

Christopher L. Jorgensen

Maple Leaf Farms, Inc.
P.O. Box 308
Milford, Indiana 46542-0308

December 10, 2012

Dear Mr. Jorgensen,

Thank you for contacting us. We are sorry your experience with duck was a traumatizing one. A former customer of ours, Hezekiah Hornsby, had a similar experience a number of years ago. Hezekiah aspired to be a world-renowned chef, inviting friends to test his new recipes. After a number of them "disappeared," Hezekiah thought it best to flee the country. Turns out, Belize makes a comparable destination for expatriates. Food for thought.

All tragedy aside, thank you for your continued loyalty to our product. Frankly, we don't see that sort of tenacity often.

Without a doubt, your younger self undercooked the duck. And incidentally, your most recent preparation was overcooked. If you are brave enough to try your hand at roasting a duck again, we would suggest watching our website's instructional duck-roasting video before preparation in order to avoid any accusations of foul play.

But if a whole duck seems too daunting, we would be more than happy to send you a couple of our fully cooked roast half ducks (also available in many grocery stores and online). Not only is it delicious, this product is so simple your in-laws can cook it. As long as you can operate an oven or grill, you should be able to prepare it without incident.

If you would like to take us up on our offer of fully cooked roast half duck, please contact us at 1-800-348-2812 so we can coordinate delivery.

Please also feel free to extend this offer to your prom date if your paths ever cross. She may have ditched duck after your date, but we would welcome the opportunity to win her back. And armed with our roast half duck, you may win her back, too.

Sincerely,

Dawn White

Christopher L. Jorgensen
P.O. Box 546
Ames, IA 50010

June 9, 2008

Abe Vigoda
Scott Stander & Associates, Inc.
13701 Riverside Drive
Suite 201
Sherman Oaks, CA 91423

Dear Mr. Vigoda,

Have you ever seen the website http://www.abevigoda.com?
I check it nearly every single day to make sure you are
still alive. I was wondering what it would be like to
have a site like this, someplace you could go if you
were ever in doubt, and just check! Is it weird to know
this is out there? If there was a christopher-
ljorgensen.com site that did this I would do nothing
but reload it over and over all day!

I guess a site like this is not as weird as hearing
that you are dead I imagine, and I read this has
happened to you more than once.

Anyway, wanted to know if you had ever been to the
site. Oh, in case you you were wondering, as of
Saturday June 9 2008 7:40:27 AM PT you are still
alive.

Sincerely,

Christopher L. Jorgensen

Christopher L. Jorgensen
P.O. Box 546
Ames, IA 50010

February 11, 2011

Duluth Trading Company
P.O. Box 200
Belleville, WI 53508-0200

Dear Duluth Trading Company,

Recently I heard a tape of President Lyndon B.
Johnson ordering a pair of pants from Joe
Haggar. The President was very specific as to
what he wanted in a pair of pants:

And another thing - the crotch, down where your
nuts hang - is always a little too tight, so
when you make them up, give me an inch that I
can let out there, uh because they cut me, it's
just like riding a wire fence. These are almost,
these are the best I've had anywhere in the
United States. But, uh when I gain a little
weight they cut me under there. So, leave me,
you never do have much of margin there. See if
you can't leave me an inch from where the zipper
ends, round, under my, back to my bunghole, so
I can let it out there if I need to.

Well, immediately I thought what the President
really needed was a pair of your Men's USA-made
5-Pocket Ballroom Jeans! (By the way I love the
"ballroom" pun!) Regardless of what Thomas
Jefferson or the Declaration of Independence
may say, not all men are created equal (if you
know what I mean!). Many of us have the exact
same problem as LBJ, many of us need your
"hidden crotch gusset." It's too bad you can't
go back in time and send LBJ a pair, but what I

thought you should do is send President Obama a pair. I'm not sure whether Obama is built like me or LBJ, but still it'd be funny, and everyone could use another pair of pants!

By the way I wear a 38/32.

Sincerely,

Christopher L. Jorgensen

p.s. I'm not sure why you have a man kicking a donkey on your website. Animal cruelty is seldom funny.

Duluth Trading Co
PO Box 409
170 Countryside Drive
Belleville, WI 53508

February 14, 2011

Dear Mr. Jorgenson:

Thank you so very much for the humorous words of your recent letter concerning our ballroom jeans. We sincerely appreciate hearing from our customers and I will be happy to forward this to our creative team. I know they will enjoy it!

I sincerely appreciate you taking time out of your busy schedule to write to us and send such a nice greeting. Thanks for making our day brighter. Please contact us if we can ever assist you further in any way.

Sincerely,

Dawn Lynch
Customer Service

Christopher L. Jorgensen
P.O. Box 546
Ames, IA 50010

October 2, 2012

Nye Labs, LLC
Bill Nye The Science Guy
4742 42nd Avenue SW, #143
Seattle, WA 98116

Dear Bill Nye,

I doubt even Jesus believed in Creationism.

Sincerely,

Christopher L. Jorgensen

p.s. can I get an autographed photo.

Christopher L. Jorgensen
P.O. Box 546
Ames, IA 50010

September 26, 2012

Mesa Tactical
1760 Monrovia Ave, #B1
Costa Mesa, CA 92627

Dear Mesa Tactical,

The other day one of my Facebook friends, Phil James,
liked your "Mesa Tactical" page on Facebook, so I
looked at what he was liking. I have to admit I didn't
get it, but then people like the stupidest shit on
Facebook. I visited your site and fell in love with
your SureShell Shotshell Carriers! Man, I wished I
lived the kind of life where owning something like this
would make sense, but honestly, I don't have kids so
my need for this would be limited. Also, as you can
see from my address I live in Iowa. We don't really
have much crime here.

Phil lives in Colorado though and from what he tells me
shit be crazy there! I don't know why he liked your
page. I am sure there is something you make that he
wants. Or maybe he already owns everything you make and
that's why he got excited you are on Facebook.

Anyway, I thought if you sent me something like a
hat or some stickers or a gun or something that would
let Phil know I was looking out for him that would
be great. I promise I'll pass it along unless it's
so cool I want to keep it for myself. It would have
to be cooler than a hat that says "Cocksucker" on it
though. I sent one of those to Phil already.

Sincerely,

Christopher L. Jorgensen

MESA TACTICAL
1760 Monrovia Ave, #B1
Costa Mesa, CA 92627

October 22, 2012

Dear Chrisotpher,

Thank you for taking the time to write us a letter. We had quite an enjoyable time reading your elaborated letter. Needless to say it was Unique and graphic.

As a Thank YOU for your letter and Support, I have included a T-shirt and Hat enclosed.

Hope they are the correct fit and hope you enjoy your Gift.

Have a great day!

Mesa Tactical Staff

*"Gear and accessories for law enforcement,
military and personal defense."*

Christopher L. Jorgensen
P.O. Box 546
Ames, IA 50010

September 9, 2010

Banana Republic
Customer Services
5900 North Meadows Drive
Grove City, OH 43123-8476

Dear Banana Republic,

I recently bought myself one of those emo
hipster Banana Republic hoodies and I do look
good in it (if I do say so myself), but I got
to looking at the tag and it says it's made with
95% cotton and 5% organic cotton. What's the
point of going organic at that point? If 95% of
the cotton isn't organic then any pesticides or
anything bad in the cotton is in 95% of my
hoodie. Now, if this formula were reversed I
obviously wouldn't be as concerned, since my
hoodie would be mostly organic. I'm just not
getting the whole mixing of cottons thing. So
what's up with this?

I try to be a socially responsible consumer, so
I'd rather have a 100% organic cotton hoodie,
but if I have to pick I'll take fashion over
substance any day!

Sincerely,

Christopher L. Jorgensen

Gap Inc.
5900 North Meadows Drive
Grove City, OH 43123
September 14, 2010

Dear Mr. Jorgensen:

Thank you for your letter to Banana Republic. We appreciate the time you've taken to share your feedback about your Banana Republic hoodie. At Banana Republic, our goal is to provide merchandise of exceptional quality and style, and we appreciate you sharing your feedback about the amount of organic cotton used in your hoodie.

We're thrilled to hear that you enjoy wearing your Emo Hipster Hoodie. We know many of our customers are interested in purchasing garments made with organic cotton. Unfortunately, demand for organic cotton has outpaced supply; there simply aren't enough organic farms operating. Additionally, turning the fibers into fabrics requires a painstaking documentation and certification process. Please be assured that we will share your feedback regarding the higher content of cotton versus organic cotton to the appropriate individuals within our company.

Than you, again for your letter Mr. Jorgensen. We look forward to shopping with you again soon.

Sincerely,

Chris Wingenfield
Gap Inc. Customer Relations

Christopher L. Jorgensen
P.O. Box 546
Ames, IA 50010

February 6, 2013

My Shreddies
38 Jubilee Drive
Loughborough,Leicestershire
LE11 5XS
UK

Dear Shreddies,

My friend Anthony Imperioli has a problem I
would like to help him with. He's Canadian and
farts a lot. There's not much to be done about
the being Canadian part, but the boy is gassier
than all get out and sometimes I think I can
smell him from here! (As you can see from my
address I live in the US.) I did a search to
see if there were any products to help Anthony
out and I found a pharmacy in China that claims
it has a pill that can make farts smell like
roses. This is too good to be true or I'd order
a bottle (Valentine's Day is coming up).
Suspecting the fart pill to be a lie I moved on
and discovered your product! Shreddies sound
nearly too good to be true, and yet plausible
enough I figured I'd order a pair and suggest
Anthony give 'em a go!

I ran into two problems. 1. I can't figure out a
way to order them in the US and have them shipped
to Canada. (While I could have some Shreddies de-
livered to me and then send them on this seems
quite inefficient and probably more expensive.)
2. You only seem to have small and medium pairs
available on your gift site. (While there's a
good chance Anthony could squeeze into a medium
I'm guessing this would put undue and

unacceptable strain on his package. I haven't
actually asked him his size--I will before
placing an order--but most real men wear at
least a large!)

Mostly I am writing you to see if you can help
me help Anthony. Or maybe you could just let me
know if the fart pill is real.

Sincerely,

Christopher L. Jorgensen

My Shreddies
LADIES' & GENTLEMAN'S UNDERWEAR
38 Jubilee Drive
Loughborough, Leicstershire,
LE11 5XS UK

19th February 2013

Dear Christopher,

Thank you very much for your letter, I have to say it made me chuckle in quite a few places.

I couldn't really comment on the Chinese pills, as this is the first I have heard of them, I will definitely look into it now though. If I find anything I will let you know.

Shreddies on the other hand do work. They contain a layer of activated carbon cloth that traps and filters all flatulence odours. This technology is also used in chemical warfare suits, so it is proven to work.

In case you aren't won over, I have included some further information for you to have a look at.

If you would like to email me with the details of your order I can take payment through PayPal rather than going through the website.

We are having a new website built, so the current one isn't displaying everything it should, as we have large in stock. Please send your email to ianthe@myshreddies.com .

Kind regards,

Miss I M Betts-Clarke.

Christopher L. Jorgensen
P.O. Box 546
Ames, IA 50010

April 15, 2008

His Holiness Pope Benedict XVI
Vaticano City
Italy

His Holiness Pope Benedict XVI,

Any way I could get an autographed photo?

You should consider bringing back the sale of
indulgences. This could be a real money maker for
for The Catholic Church! I'm thinking only for
venial sins, but that's really your call.

This might help offset some of the financial
losses due to the ongoing sex abuse scandals in
the United States and elsewhere. Think about it.

I am enclosing one United States Dollar for the
impure thoughts I constantly have. I doubt if this
is enough money for them all, but it's the gesture
that counts, right?

Thanks,

Christopher L. Jorgensen

p.s. I heard that muslims now outnumber
catholics. Does the Vatican have a plan to
encourage more catholic women to have more
babies? Perhaps it is time to allow priests
and nuns to get married (not to each other of
course, that would obviously be wrong).

enc: $1

Christopher L. Jorgensen
P.O. Box 546
Ames, IA 50010

September 27, 2010

National Geographic Society
1145 17th Street N.W.
Washington, D.C. 20036-4688

Dear National Geographic,

I think you should come out with an issue
with nothing but naked women in it. Bear
with me here. Many adult men had their first
glimpse of a woman's naked breasts (that's
not their mother's) from viewing your magazine. In fact multiple generations of men grew
up seeking furtive glimpses of nudity in
your magazine. I remember doing this in grade
school!

Now, I am not talking anything as tasteless
as a "Girls of National Geographic," but something that taps into that sense of nostalgia
many an adult male has would be wonderful!
In this age of the internet--where pretty
much anything can be seen with a click--
coming out with a magazine like this would
serve to fill a void: man as animal in her
natural state.

You can feel free to do a men's issue as
well, but this won't be as interesting to me.

Sincerely,

Christopher L. Jorgensen

National Geographic
1145 17th Street N.W.
Washington, D.C. 20036-4688

Thank you for contacting the National Geographic Society.

Suggestions from our readers play an important role as we plan future coverage. I have forwarded your suggestion along to the appropriate editorial specialist for consideration. Bear in mind, however, that because we are only able to publish about 70 articles per year, only the most promising ideas are considered.

Thank you for your interest in the National Geographic Society and its work.

Christopher L. Jorgensen
P.O. Box 546
Ames, IA 50010

January 26, 2012

Bush Brothers and Co.
PO Box 52330, Department C
Knoxville, TN 37950-2330

Dear Bush Beans,

This is going to be a strange story, but I swear it's true. My girlfriend's cat loves chickpea jelly from your garbanzo beans cans. She eats up the stuff and begs for more. We feed it to her using a special spatula reserved solely for her use. We call this the cat spatula! It's so bad that when we make something that comes in a can, but isn't garbanzo beans, she insists on inspecting the can to make sure we're not holding out on her.

For Christmas I got my girlfriend's cat a can of Bush Brothers chickpeas and the inaugural issue of "Chickpea" magazine. I put these in her stocking above the fire-place (my girlfriend made the cat's stocking and it is red and green and shaped like a paw!). She wasn't that impressed, but she's a cat. She can't read (yet) and can't open the can on her own (yet), so I don't know what reaction I should have been expecting.

We plan to shoot video of her enjoying her chickpea jelly treat off her cat spatula! If you're interested I can send you a link to the video if I ever figure out YouTube. The cat's name is Honey Quow. (There's a story

there too, but it's too long and I have
things to do today.)

Would it be possible to get a can of the
chickpea jelly without the garbanzo beans?

Sincerely,

Christopher L. Jorgensen

Bush's Best
Bush Brothers & Company
1016 East Weisgarber Road
Knoxville, TN 37909-2669

January 31, 2012

Dear Mr. Jorgensen:

Thank you for complimenting our Garbanzo Beans. We are delighted to hear that you and your cat have tried and enjoyed our products.

We do not package our products without beans...it is actually the natural starch from the beans that thicken the brine in the can - without the beans, it would only be water and salt.

Again, we thank you for taking the time to contact us. We appreciate your interest in our products.

Sincerely,

Kenna Hess
Consumer Relations Coordinator

Enclosures :
(2) Variety Beans ¢ Off

Christopher L. Jorgensen
P.O. Box 546
Ames, IA 50010

May 1, 2008

Federal Bureau of Investigation
J. Edgar Hoover Building
935 Pennsylvania Avenue, NW
Washington, D.C. 20535-0001

Dear FBI,

Is it true you keep a file on every US citizen?
Can I request mine and my girlfriend's? I'd just
like to see what you have to say about us. I'd
tell you her name, but I'm sure you already know
that, since we've been dating for some time now.

Also, anyway I can get a list of all the lists
I am on?

Thanks,

Christopher L. Jorgensen

Christopher L. Jorgensen
P.O. Box 546
Ames, IA 50010

December 14, 2009

Citizens' Stamp Advisory Committee
U.S. Postal Service
1735 North Lynn St. Suite 5013
Arlington, VA 22209-6432

Dear Stamp Development People,

I know planning and approving and putting out
a stamp takes a lot more time and work than
anyone probably gives you credit for. First,
I'd like to thank you for all your hard work
and time spent making wonderful stamps (I
particularly like the self adhesive ones).
So thanks!

I have a great idea for a stamp. Perhaps
you've heard of poet and novelist Charles
Bukowski? Well, it's coming on 20 years since
his death (March 9, 2014), and since you put
notable people on stamps it seems to me he'd
be perfect to put on a commemorative U.S.
postal stamp. This gives you a little over 4
years to approve this idea, hire an artist,
and get this stamp painted! I think you can
do it. I have faith in you!

Bukowski even wrote a book about working in a
post office called "Post Office" (he's often more
creative than this). If you won't give the man
his stamp, you should at least read this book.
I think it should be required reading for every
postman, but then I am uncertain how well women
postmen would like it.

If a Charles Bukowski is out of the question, what about Dennis J. Kucinich? He'd be cool too.

Sincerely,

Christopher L. Jorgensen

United States Postal Service
Stamp Services
1735 N Lynn Street
Suite 5013
Arlington, VA 22209-6432

Thank you for your recent correspondence. Each year, the Postal Service receives thousands of suggestions for new postage stamps. As the number of stamps we issue is limited, the Citizens' Stamp Advisory Committee was established in 1957 to review all suggestions and make recommendations for new stamps to the Postmaster General. The Committee members base their recommendations on national interest, historical perspective, and other criteria.

There is no specific time frame for the issuance of stamps featuring a particular subject. The Committee decides on new stamp subjects two to three years in advance of the issue date in order to provide lead-time for planning, designing, production, and distribution. Although many of the subjects for upcoming stamps have been identified, no public announcement is made until the entire philatelic program for that year has been approved. This normally occurs in the fall preceding the year of issuance.

Your comments are being included in the Committee's files.

Christopher L. Jorgensen
P.O. Box 546
Ames, IA 50010

April 22, 2011

John D. and Catherine T. MacArthur Foundation
140 S. Dearborn Street
Chicago, IL 60603-5285

Dear John D. and Catherine T.,

First, I want to thank you for your ongoing support
of NPR. Sadly, I agree with those who believe NPR
should not receive government funding, because
accepting a check compromises perception of
independence and integrity, but for NPR to be fully
funded by the people then those that use this
service need to step up. I thank you for going
above and beyond in this respect.

I am also wanting to bring to your attention
"Dilbert" creator Scott Adams. He has been running
around calling himself a genius. I've checked your
role of grant recipients and either he is wrong or
you've overlooked listing him. He says he's been
certified as a genius, but I'm just not seeing it.

Usually when people say they are a genius they come
off as being pretty annoying, which is why it's a
good thing your foundation is out there to ring that
bell for these people! The way I figure it either
Scott Adams is a genius and you probably owe him a
check, or he's just some jerk running around
pretending to be cooler than he is.

I figured I'd ask the experts. Is Scott Adams a genius?

Sincerely,

Christopher L. Jorgensen

Christopher L. Jorgensen
P.O. Box 546
Ames, IA 50010

January 8, 2009

Avery's Beverages
520 Corbin Ave.
New Britain, CT 06052

Dear Avery's Beverages,

I thought about ordering a few cases of your
"Kitty Piddle Soda" as a gag gift (pun intended!), but then I saw how much it costs to ship.
$1.25 a bottle? Do you guys think you are Pepsi!

But then, thankfully, I noticed you have "Make
Your Own Soda" tours. And I though, "I could do
that!" Connecticut is a bit far for me to travel
though (and there's the whole not being allowed
out of the state thing), so a tour is out for me.
"How hard can it be?" I asked myself. And once
asked I had to find out.

Damn hard is the answer! I've been following my
cat around for 3 days now and haven't managed
to get even one 12 oz. bottle even a third full.
Can you send me some tips on how best to do
this? Do I just need more cats?

Thanks for all your help,

Christopher L. Jorgensen

Avery's Beverages
520 Corbin Ave.
New Britain, CT 06052

Dear Mr. Jorgensen:

Thanks so much for your letter regarding our Kitty Piddle Soda. I certainly can understand your tribulations in attempting to replicate our popular soda. We wouldn't usually divulge our secret recipes and manufacturing methods, but your letter touched us and we decided to make an exception.

As you probably have discerned by now, you need more cats. The local animal shelter is a good source for additional felines, although there is some competition from the crazy cat lady and Mr. Lee from Peking Palace. Once you reach your critical kitty mass you need to work on hydration. We over saturate the little fur balls to the point that they slosh when they walk, giving the added benefit that they are much easier to catch in this condition. The next step is to have the cats ingest large quantities of sweets until their little pancreas's shut down (this saves us the step of having to add additional sugar to the final product). The final step is carbonation. We have chosen to achieve our carbonation through natural methods (like fine champagne) and add a little yeast to their diets. Please be very careful with the yeast dosage, as we had some very unfortunate accidents early on. You can't imagine the mess that thirty-some exploding cats can make!

Once you have mastered the manufacturing nuances of Kitty Piddle Soda you may want to challenge yourself to try our popular Dog Drool Soda. Ernie Pavlov is our production manager for that soda line and I am sure that he would be happy to share some of his techniques with you. One tip that I might share, is that if you intend to use free range cats and dogs (as we do) it is a good idea to have separate facilities for the two operations. Even though the yield from our kitty piddle operation increased impressively when we added the dogs, we had a few messy incidents which set us back a bit. Best of luck with your efforts, please keep us posted on your progress.

Kindest regards,

Rob Metz
Chief Bottle Washer

Christopher L. Jorgensen
P.O. Box 546
Ames, IA 50010

December 9, 2008

Amnesty International
5 Penn Plaza, 16th Floor
New York, NY 10001

Dear Amnesty International,

Does this letter writing stuff really work?
Seems to me it wouldn't be very effective. If I
were a despot or part of a malicious illegit-
imate regime, and I was torturing people and
denying them basic human rights, then the last
thing I'd really care about was opening my mail!
I'd probably just force other people to do that
for me! (As an evil dictator why should I risk
paper cuts?)

I'm not sure if I get the point of the whole
letter writing thing. If I write someone bad
should I expect my letter will be considered
and wait for a reply? Are the letters ever
answered?

Sincerely,

Christopher L. Jorgensen

Amnesty International USA
5 Penn Plaza, 16th Fl
New York, NY 10010-1810

Dear Christopher Jorgensen:

Thanks for your letter of inquiry about the effectiveness of Amnesty International's campaigning. Sometimes we get the results we want, sometimes not, but we believe that government officials do care about their image and may respond to organized pressure. I'm sending you a bunch of print-outs from our website, in case you don't have a computer. You can see some of the many ways, big and small, that we can protect people's human rights.

Sometimes people get answers to their letters, but mostly not. Our objective is showing authorities that concerned men and women from countries all over the world are watching their actions, and urging them to abide by their own laws and uphold the basic rights of their citizens.

Sincerely,

Beth Ross

Christopher L. Jorgensen
P.O. Box 546
Ames, IA 50010

April 18, 2008

Asshat Jan Mickelson
WHO Radio
2141 Grand Avenue
Des Moines, IA 50312-5230

Dear Asshat,

I think you are a facist and a bigot. I hate
your show. You're Limbaugh Lite; none of the
humor, and half the intelligence. You're an
idiot. If you weren't so stupid you'd know that
already.

Sincerely,

Christopher L. Jorgensen

p.s. Any way I can get an autographed photo?

Christopher L. Jorgensen
P.O. Box 546
Ames, IA 50010

December 14, 2010

Peaceful Valley Donkey Rescue
PO Box 2210
Tehachapi, CA 93581

Dear Peaceful Valley Donkey Rescue,

Merry Christmas!

Here's $5! I realize it's not a lot, but then I
don't have a lot to give. I thought of sticking
it into some skywalk musician's case, but
honestly most of those guys aren't any good.
Their songs are poorly disguised institution-
alized begging! If anything I've considered
offering them money to quit playing, but I don't
think $5 is enough to get them to stop, and I
don't want to hurt anyone's feelings. If it wasn't
so damn cold out I'd go outside to avoid these
guys. I find myself thinking, "They're so bad I'd
rather give my money to a donkey!" I know people
think shit like this all the time, but I bet few
of them follow through. Well I do! So here's $5.

I wanted to explain why I am sending money to
a donkey rather than giving it to one of those
undeserving people! Please select a worthy
jackass and buy him something special.

Sorry I vented. Thanks for listening!

Sincerely,

Christopher L. Jorgensen

ABOUT THE AUTHOR

Christopher L. Jorgensen has been on the Earth for over 40 years. It is unknown how many years he's spent on other planets as a Space Marine.

Nearly everything that needs said about this man has already been said. But who said you had to have a need before saying something? This book is proof this just isn't the case.

During his deformative years Christopher was exposed to too much SCTV, constant late night HBO showings of "Excalibur" and "Altered States," and countless live matches of Jai alai (it's big in Iowa).

In his ample spare time he likes to create recipes for puppy and to pursue new hobbies. He owns more domain names than you can shake a stick at!

His girlfriend/editor/typist would prefer you not encourage him (that's her job).

ACKNOWLEDGEMENTS

A project like *Jackass Letters* really wouldn't be possible without the ongoing help of others.

First, I thank the girlfriend/editor/typist since she's stuck by me for a decade, and I really would have given up on *jackassletters.com* if I'd had to do it all alone. Second, I thank Marc J. Randazza for being my lawyer, answering my stupid legal questions, and for permitting the girlfriend/editor/typist to sleep mostly soundly at night. And lastly, I thank Anthony Imperioli. He really is an inspiration and my muse. Anthony does the illustrations on the website and is a good sport when it comes to being a character in the letters.

This list is probably not exhaustive, so if you helped out in some way, and I failed to thank you, then thank you.

CPSIA information can be obtained
at www.ICGtesting.com
Printed in the USA
LVOW05s2218160217

524568LV00006B/403/P